WATERS FOR THE THIRSTY SOUL™

To Ngozi & Ken,

May God continually bless you and keep you safe. Amen.

[illegible]

Dec 2019.

WATERS FOR THE THIRSTY SOUL™

52 refreshing truths to deepen your relationship with God

OGE FUNLOLA MODIE

Prestige

Published in Nigeria in 2018 by Kachifo Limited
Under its Prestige imprint
253 Herbert Macaulay Way
Yaba, Lagos, Nigeria
0807 736 4217
info@prestige.ng
www.prestige.ng

A catalogue record for this book is available from the National Library of Nigeria.

ISBN: 978-978-55721-2-4

Layout and cover design by Akeem Ibrahim

CONTENTS

FOREWORD

From an early age, I observed Oge Modie's hunger and thirst for the things of God through her active involvement in the Sunday School of the Chapel of Redemption at the University of Nigeria Enugu Campus. I also noticed Oge's boldness and courage when she freely shared her faith and first love with her classmates throughout her educational pursuits. Over our past four decades of friendship, I have gained an immense respect for her walk with God.

Of her many gifts, I would argue that Oge's greatest gift is her generous spirit. Oge shares everything that she has with others. Her home is a shelter and refuge to many and she caters for the needs of orphans, widows, the youth and countless children. She also freely shares her love for God and the insights that she has gained as an apostle in corporate Nigeria and, more recently, in public service through her blog, the Wellspring of Life, her radio show, and by hosting monthly prayer sessions in Abuja.

This devotional, *Waters for the Thirsty Soul*, is yet another gift from Oge to the world, through which she shares unique insights into the nature of God and the

abundant life that He promises to those who diligently seek him. The choice of her themes – from love and joy to trials and God's will – demonstrate Oge's appreciation of the challenges and triumphs of the Christian walk, and her commitment to providing practical insights for everyday people. The structure of each chapter, with an in-depth review of the theme, the prayer and then the charge, provides a complete nourishing and refreshing drink of God's Word for those who thirst.

Waters for the Thirsty Soul, with its "52 refreshing truths to deepen your relationship with God" is a welcome addition to the Christian's toolkit and will provide wisdom, direction and insights for those who are seeking to be filled by God. This book is the first of many devotionals and books that Oge will share with us as she continues to unveil her many gifts and her unique insight into the Word of and ways of God for the world to learn, grow and enjoy!

Ndidi Okonkwo Nwuneli (MFR)
Fellow co-labourer in God's vineyard
Founder, LEAP Africa
Co-Founder, AACE Foods
Managing Partner, Sahel Consulting

INTRODUCTION

Waters for the Thirsty Soul™ is inspired by the story of the Samaritan woman found in the fourth chapter of the book of John. I have often wondered about the phrase, "living life abundantly", pulled from that text, especially how the concept seems elusive to many believers.

The word "abundance" speaks of a state of plenty – having all things sufficient and living life fully. However, at times, it seems the realities of life create circumstances that make us question Christ's promise of the abundant life. In explaining His mission on earth, Jesus said, "The thief's mission is *to steal, kill and destroy*, but I have come to give them life, and to give them more abundantly." In other words, Christ came to **give us life** and to help us **live life in abundance** (live life to the full).

There was a time I felt God had abandoned me. I wanted no part of being a believer even though I had been a believer since I was nine years old. Then, it seemed that God had looked away when my dad was murdered, so I felt alone and wondered about the relevance of being a Christian. That was when the Holy Spirit took me to the story of the Samaritan woman.

But whoever drinks the water I give them will never thirst. Indeed, the water I give them will become in them a spring of water welling up to eternal life." **John 4:14(NIV)**

I realised that the "abundant life" could only be found in daily personal encounters with Jesus Christ. It could only take a one-on-one encounter with Him, just like with the Samaritan woman. The life Christ offered was life in Him, eternally dwelling in us through the Holy Spirit. This abundant life transcends the physical. Life can be hard, but you can experience a deep-seated stability despite this because of the eternal life you have in Christ.

This devotional shares bits of my encounters with Jesus as I read the account of the Samaritan woman.

So join me. Take a drink of what Jesus offers and become emboldened to live life in abundance.

HOW TO USE THIS DEVOTIONAL

Each devotional comes with a theme, a prayer and a charge. The theme allows you to capture the essence of the message, the scripture and the relevance to everyday life.

The prayer is designed as a start to many other prayers to be said to build the individual's relationship/walk with Christ.

The charge is a call to action on the part of the individual. Faith without works is dead. The charge puts faith to work.

Bible Translations

NIV	New International Version
MSG	Message Bible
NKJV	New King James Version
KJV	King James Version
NLT	New Living Translation

LOVE

For God so loved the world that He gave His one and only Son, that whoever believes in Him shall not perish but have eternal life.

JOHN 3:16 (NIV)

FOUR WAYS TO LOVE GOD

Our Lord Jesus Christ captured the essence of the Ten Commandments in two key philosophies: love God and love your neighbour as yourself. The first four mandates of the Ten Commandments instruct us to love God. God loves us and desires that we shower our affections on Him.

> *And you shall love the Lord your God with all your heart, with all your soul, with all your mind and with all your strength. This is the first commandment.* **Mark 12:30(NKJV)**

The four ways to love God are: with all your heart, your soul, your mind and your strength.

To love God with all your heart is to love Him with passion. Our actions showcase the state of our heart. How much do you love God? How passionate are you about God? How eager are you to showing God off? How much do you desire God?

To love God with all your soul is to love Him with your life. It could also be to devote yourself to Him in the

place of prayer. How often do you communicate with God? Only in troubled times? What does your life speak of? Righteousness? Holiness? Does your lifestyle speak of His love?

To love God with all your mind is to love Him with all your intelligence, i.e. your faculty of thought and moral understanding. Our thoughts can define our lifestyle or attitude towards God and people. Do we let our thoughts drive our definition of God and His ways?

To love God with all your strength is to love Him with your whole energy. There are mornings it will take all of your strength to say a prayer and days when everything seems to go wrong and your praise takes a hike. Yet, when you love God with all your energy, you will lift a song of praise up to him. You will stay true to your purpose.

In summary, love the Lord your God with all your passion, prayer, intelligence and energy. This is a very clear command from God and, indeed, He is our greatest reward. Step into this amazing love affair and enjoy the goodness of the Lord.

Prayer:

Oh Lord, help me to totally obey your first and most important commandment, to love you with all my heart, mind, soul and strength. In Jesus' name. Amen!

Charge:

I charge you to hurry into the holy of holies to pour your love on Him.

WHY YOU CAN'T LOVE OTHERS

The month of February is celebrated across the world as the month of love. However, as we profess love to people, the question is, do we really know what it means to love others?

> *And here is the second: "Love others as well as you love yourself."* **Mark 12:31(MSG)**

Love others as well as you love yourself. This simply means you can only give the love you have. If you don't love yourself, you will be unable to love others. Do you have a selfish vain love for self or a love that truly cares about your state of being? What value have you placed on yourself? Through His actions, God modelled the true meaning of love. John 3:16 states that "God so loved the world (you) that He gave His only begotten Son." In other words, God gave us His best. That's the extent of His love. Jesus also gave His life for us so that we may be reconciled to the Father. What a wonderful love! The first step to loving ourselves is recognising and accepting

the love of the Father through Jesus Christ. A closer walk with God, born out of a deep commitment to knowing and loving Him, also helps us see ourselves as God sees us. As we see and love ourselves in Christ, we are able to extend love to others.

Abusive relationships, failed marriages and traumatic childhood memories may have perverted the way we view ourselves. We may have carried some faulty perceptions of ourselves into our daily interactions, and consequently, treated others unfairly. Today, shake off that perverted view. Look at yourself through the loving eyes of the Father and start to appreciate your beautiful and wonderfully-made self. You are unique and created for signs and wonders. When you start to love yourself as God loves you, you will begin to treat others as well as you treat yourself.

Prayer:

Father, please help me to see myself as you see me. Open my eyes afresh to this wonder. In Jesus' name. Amen!

Charge:

Learn to love yourself. Seek a deeper walk with God. Do not fear! Open yourself up for spiritual surgery/circumcision. Let God cut away all limitations to loving yourself in Christ Jesus.

MONEY CANNOT BUY (TRUE) LOVE

True love comes from God and He teaches us by His Spirit how to love and accept each other. The concept of money and love is one that has bothered me for some time. There is a popular saying that "money cannot buy **true** love". I emphasise "true" because money can certainly buy deception, lies and falsehood masquerading as love.

> *Love is invincible facing death and danger. Passion laughs at the terrors of hell. The fire of love stops at nothing – it sweeps everything before it. Flood waters can't drown love, torrents of rain can't put it out. Love can't be bought, love can't be sold – it's not to be in the marketplace.* **Songs of Solomon 8:7 (MSG)**

Love is action. The only example of true love is found in our Heavenly Father. God's pattern of love is about giving your best and expecting nothing in return. John 3:16a says, "This is how much God loved the world: He

gave his Son, His one and only Son." He gave us Jesus Christ when we were still sinners. It was a big risk, not knowing if we will accept Jesus, yet hoping that we will, so we can come into a covenant relationship with Him. That is true love. It is about hoping for the best in and for someone. The idea that spending money on people can induce them to love you is a misconception. When you function in God's kind of love, giving of yourself and your resources will become a way of life and become more meaningful to both you and the receiver. Remember the Word of God says, "It is more blessed to give than to receive." We must submit ourselves to the Holy Spirit daily, so He can work in us to love God's way. That's the only way to love and be joyful in spite of the response or attitude of the receiver.

Paul gives us a definition of the God kind of love in I Corinthians 13. My best part of this charge is found in verse three – "If I give everything I own to the poor and even go to the stake to be burned as a martyr, but I don't love, I have gotten nowhere. So, no matter what I say, what I believe, and what I do, I'm bankrupt without love." Money can't buy love; rather, with all the money you have, you are bankrupt without love.

Prayer:

Father, teach me to love Your way, in Jesus' name I pray. Amen.

Charge:

Loving God's way is supernatural. You can't achieve this by yourself. So today, let the Holy Spirit spread His love in your heart, that you may love people the way God loves.

JOY

Then he said to them, "Go your way, eat the fat, drink the sweet, and send portions to those for whom nothing is prepared; for this day is holy to our Lord. Do not sorrow, for the joy of the Lord is your strength."

NEHEMIAH 8:10 (NKJV)

THE FRUIT CALLED JOY

There are quite a few things in life that seem not to matter until they are lost. One of such is joy. We know that the eternal things, the priceless things of life are not tangible, and thus are unequalled to the tangible. This is why money may buy you luxury but can't guarantee joy, just as it can buy a good bed but not good sleep.

But the fruit of the Spirit is love, joy, peace, forbearance, kindness, goodness, faithfulness, gentleness and self-control. Against such things there is no law. **Galatians 5:22-23**

Joy is a fruit of the spirit. It does not rely on the physical environment or the realities of what life throws in your face. It is grown in the Spirit and accessible to the spiritual being in Christ. Thus, it is irreplaceable, incomparable, intangible yet so free!

Being a fruit means a seed has to be sown. The incorruptible seed of Christ is sown in our hearts once we accept Him as our personal Lord and Saviour. As we spend time in the presence of the Father, we receive joy. The word of God says, "In the presence of God is the full-

ness of Joy and at His right hand are pleasures evermore." Bearing fruits of joy require staying in God's presence. Joy is a strength builder during trials and tough times.

The indwelling of the Holy Spirit is key to our bearing fruits of the Spirit and staying victorious daily. Joy promotes a life of thanksgiving and gratitude. Being joyful takes you beyond the bane of just surviving to thriving. God, being omniscient (all-knowing) has wisely hidden these precious things in our spirit where it is untouchable by the enemy. **Ephesians 1:3**

Joy also promotes good health and right thinking. Joy will help you see through the tears and heartbreak, knowing that God is for you. Joy exhibits strength in the face of opposition and war. Joy is a fruit that is critical to our spiritual growth and kingdom advancement.

Today, stay in God's presence. Receive joy immeasurable.

Prayer:

Dear Lord, I desire to dwell in your presence all the days of my life. I want to drink of You and receive immeasurable joy. Strengthen me with Your joy. In Jesus' name. Amen.

Charge:

Choose to be joyful in spite of the situation. Be led by the Holy Spirit. Only through Him can we bear the fruit of joy daily.

JOY IN THE MORNING

Seasons of trials create a trail of tears. Frustrated at the twists and turns of life, we often give up on God and ourselves. Be encouraged today; there is a timeline to every challenge you face.

> *Weeping may stay for the night, but rejoicing comes in the morning.* **Psalm 30:5b**

The scripture above tells us God has given timelines to everything. What separates the night from the morning is the sun rising! "For the Sun of Righteousness shall arise with healing on His wings." The intervention of Jesus in the night brings joy in the morning. His presence soothes and repairs the broken. His power sets the captives free. His touch makes the sick well. Jesus Christ is the Bright Morning Star. His light chases away the darkness and brings joy.

The morning is revealed by the light of the sun as its rays gently kiss the skies and gradually reveal the beauty of the earth. This symbolises how Christ (the Sun of

Righteousness) intervenes in our dark seasons and brings joy in the morning to the believer. I will show two forms He takes:

The Form of the Word: When we speak the Word of God to our circumstances, it brings hope. Hope translates to faith and faith translates to joy.

The Form of Light: Christ is light. Light brings illumination, it brings clarity, it exposes all things, it brightens and it gives understanding.

So be encouraged! That trial has a timeline. Joy comes with the rising of the sun. The Lord is near to all that call on Him. He has come. The Light has brought deliverance. Be still. The Lord is right there with you. Alleluia!

Prayer:

Dear Father, I thank You for You have turned my mourning into dancing. *You have taken off my sackcloth and clothed me with joy.* **Psalm 30:11-12**

Charge:

Let the morning bring me the word of your unfailing love, for I have put my trust in You. Show me the way I should go, for to You I entrust my life. **Psalm 143:8**

STRENGTH BUILDING

Our daily lives require grace and strength to grow daily in the Spirit. Trials and hard times knock us down and take a lot of strength from us. We need strength day by day to continue in purpose and truth.

> *Then he said to them, "Go your way, eat the fat, drink the sweet, and send portions to those for whom nothing is prepared; for this day is holy to our Lord. Do not sorrow, for the joy of the Lord is your strength.* **Nehemiah 8:10 (NKJV)**

Joy is a fruit of the Spirit and is required for daily victorious living. It also requires staying in the presence of the Lord so that the fullness of joy is received from the Father. God expects us to know that He is for us and desires that we keep winning in this journey of life. Many times, we find it challenging to find joy in the midst of sad and terrible ordeals. However, the text today encourages us that to keep at life despite what is thrown our way, we need to stay in the presence of God to build strength to remain victorious.

His joy is the true way of building strength daily. Where do we find His joy? In His presence! Rather than move away from God during times of trial, this is the time to embrace and stay in His presence.

What do you do when in His presence? Be expectant through expressions of love, worship and praise. These expressions build a deeper relationship with the Father. As you stay in His presence, He fills you with joy. He strengthens you and helps you build faith and trust in Him.

Prayer:

Father, today I receive Your joy. Your word says the joy of the Lord is my strength. I stand on this word today. I receive strength to go on and ahead.

Charge:

Be joyful in affliction. Be joyful in the midst of affliction. Build joy through by staying in God's presence, as it is written: *So be truly glad. There is wonderful joy ahead, even though you must endure many trials for a little while.* **1 Peter 1:6**

TRIALS

"Therefore, since we are surrounded by such a great cloud of witnesses, let us throw off everything that hinders and the sin that so easily entangles. And let us run with perseverance the race marked out for us, fixing our eyes on Jesus, the pioneer and perfecter of faith. For the joy set before him he endured the cross, scorning its shame, and sat down at the right hand of the throne of God."

HEBREWS 12:1-2 (NIV)

THE HOLY SPIRIT – OUR HELPER

We often find ourselves in difficult situations, faced with challenges nearly impossible to cope with. These challenges could be physical, emotional, spiritual, mental and so on. When you feel helpless, you may wonder if life is worth it. Or you may think life is unfair. However, today, be joyful because in Christ we have help. Yes, the Holy Spirit. Alleluia!

> *And I will ask the Father, and He will give you another Helper, to be with you forever – the Spirit of Truth, whom the world cannot receive [and take to its heart] because it does not see Him or know Him, but you know Him because He (The Holy Spirit) remains with you continually and will be in you.*
> **John 14:16-17 (AMP)**

The Holy Spirit is our Helper. He is our ever-present help in times of trouble, our Comforter in times of sorrow, our Chief Advocate, our primary intercessor. He is also our Chief Life Strategist, Counsellor General, Chief Cheerleader, Strengthener of feeble knees and weak

hands. The Holy Spirit is all a believer needs to excel in life as a child of God. He demonstrates God's love for us through the working out of our daily needs and filling us with power and joy!

Recognising the Holy Spirit as the essence of Christ and knowing that having the Spirit of God in us comes with these benefits, we need not fear in times of crisis. This knowledge should give us the confidence to face life's challenges with the assurance that we will come out victorious. The Bible (in Paul's letter to the Hebrews) talks about how Jesus Christ himself was tempted in every way, like we are always tempted. But He never yielded to temptations. This was possible by the power of the Holy Spirit.

Prayer:

Dear Father, I thank you for the blessing of having the Holy Spirit dwelling in me. Thank You because He guides me in wisdom to do Your perfect will.

Charge:

It is very important that we recognise the ministry of the Holy Spirit in our lives. Walking with Him is the key to a successful life in Christ.

THROUGH THE FIRE

One of the ways our relationship (driven by faith, love and trust) with God can be deepened is through trials. Going through trials may be challenging but it is needful. It builds your relationship with God.

> *My brethren, count it all joy when you fall into various trials, knowing that the testing of your faith produces patience. But let patience have its perfect work, that you may be perfect and complete, lacking nothing.* **James 1:2-4 (NKJV)**

There are two key reasons why you should go through the trials. The first is for growth. You may sometimes wonder how any person can be happy when faced with diverse trials. It could be a terminal illness, unpaid debts, loss of money, jobs or a spouse etc. Nevertheless, the book of James reminds us to be joyful when these situations arise. Why? Because trials are a means to an end *(*see verse four*)*. Trials build trust in your relationship with God, knowing that He loves you and is *working out* the best end to that trial.

The second is that God has made you fireproof and waterproof! So what are you afraid of? In Isaiah 43:2 God says, "When you go through deep waters, I will be with you. When you go through rivers of difficulty, you will not drown. When you walk through the fire of oppression, you will not be burned up; the flames will not consume you." (NLT)

The fire of trials is to refine and burn away every impurity that has held you bound. Look at the three young Hebrew boys who were thrown into the furnace. First, the fire did not burn them. Instead, the only things that were melted in the fire were the ropes that held them bound. Second, Christ was in the fire with them (Daniel 3:25). This episode is an analogy to the verse in Isaiah and to let you know that no trial is enough to sink you. Rather you are to sink every trial through the power of Christ in you.

Today, welcome every trial with joy, knowing that God is refining and making you perfectly complete and lacking nothing. Be joyful because God allows trials to mould you into all that He wants you to be.

Prayer:

Father, I give You thanks for the trials of yesterday, today and tomorrow. I thank You because You are doing good work in me. Thank You Father as You give me grace to bear up. Open my eyes to see as You see, open my ears to hear You and please give me a heart to obey every instruction given by the Holy Spirit in this time. Amen.

Charge:

Be joyful! You are FIREPROOF and WATERPROOF! It's all working out for your good.

ENCOURAGING WORDS FROM THE FATHER – THROUGH THE FIRE

In the previous chapters, we explored the themes of personal relationship with the Father as well as going through trials. This chapter will go in-depth on the concept of going **through the fire** and becoming everything the Lord has proposed for our lives. Let us begin with the scriptures that speak of our Father's goodness through the fire.

He says:

- **It is for Good**: James 1:2-4 (NKJV) says, "My brethren, count it all joy when you fall into various trials, knowing that the testing of your faith produces patience. But let patience have its perfect work, that you may be perfect and complete, lacking nothing."

- **God Has Made You Fireproof and Waterproof:** In Isaiah 43:2 (NLT) God says, "When you go through deep waters, I will be with you. When you go through rivers of difficulty, you will not drown.

When you walk through the fire of oppression, you will not be burned up; the flames will not consume you."

Also, Jeremiah 29:11-13 (NIV) says, "For I know the plans I have for you," declares the Lord, "plans to prosper you and not to harm you, plans to give you hope and a future."

- **You are not Alone:** In Daniel 3:25(KJV), "He answered and said, Lo, I see four men loose, walking in the midst of the fire, and they have no hurt; and the form of the fourth is like the Son of God."

- **Be Bold, No Fear Here!** Deuteronomy 31:6 (NIV) says, "Be strong and courageous. Do not be afraid or terrified because of them, for the LORD your God goes with you; He will never leave you nor forsake you."

- **There is a Reward:** James 1:12 (KJV) says, "Blessed is the man that endureth temptation, for when he is tried, he shall receive the crown of life which the Lord hath promised to them that love him."

Also, in Galatians 6:9 (KJV) the Bible says, "And let us not be weary in well doing, for in due season we shall reap, if we faint not."

Check out Hebrews 10:35-36 (NKJV) as well –

"Therefore, do not throw away your confidence, which has a great reward. For you have need of endurance, so that when you have done the will of God, you may receive what was promised."

So, if there is anything to deduce from God's heart in these scriptures, it is this: it is for good. God has made you fireproof and waterproof. You are not alone. Be bold and have no fear here in the fire. There is a reward for you.

Prayer:

Father, I am thankful for Your words that comfort me through the fire. I am strengthened in You, knowing that this trial is working patience in me.

Charge:

Meditate on the scriptures shared and their interpretations. Make a note and be joyful.

THE ULTIMATE DISPLACER

Worry is detrimental to our well-being and to our relationship with God. Everyday worries can become the center of our lives and cloud our view of God.

> *Don't fret or worry. Instead of worrying, pray. Let petitions and praises shape your worries into prayers, letting God know your concerns. Before you know it, a sense of God's wholeness, everything coming together for good, will come and settle you down. It's wonderful what happens when Christ displaces worry at the center of your life.* **Philippians 4: 6-7 (MSG)**

I remember learning about displacement reaction during my chemistry classes in school. It is the process *where a compound displaces a less reactive metal from the solutions of its compounds*. In simpler terms, when a higher element comes in contact with a lesser element, it displaces it from its own combination. The Holy Spirit used this analogy to remind me of the ultimate worry displacer—Christ Jesus. The verse above aptly explains what happens when

Christ comes into contact with our worries. He displaces them and becomes the center of our lives.

So using the chemistry example,

Jesus + Oge's Worries = Jesus Oge + Worries

So you have worries, and probably valid ones too! However, you must let Jesus come into the equation. When He becomes your focal point, your worries take a back seat and you set your gaze on Him who is able to deliver and walk you through that rough time. So, does the cancer go away? Or the financial drought or the failing marriage or the sick kids? Probably not, but they will no longer remain your focus. The presence of Jesus will remind you of what the word of God says regarding your circumstance.

Today, let your heart be blessed by this ultimate displacer of our worries. Let us bring Christ in contact with our trials through our praise-filled requests and prayers, and wait faithfully for His deliverance.

Prayer:

Jesus, today I praise you for being the ultimate displacer of worries in my life. I thank you for every opportunity to bring my worries to you. I lay it all down at your feet. I believe You Lord. Jesus, be the center of my life. Amen!

Charge:

I Thessalonians 5: 16-18. Choose today to be cheerful regardless of your circumstances. Pray about everything. Everything! Be thankful no matter what happens. That is how God desires that we spend our day!

HIS TRANSFORMATION AGENDA - BREAK, MELT, MOULD AND FILL

God has a transformation agenda for everyone. Daily, God wants to transform us into His image and likeness. His desire is that we become like Jesus every day, living life abundantly and walking in purpose.

But now, O Lord, You are our Father; we are the clay, and You our potter, and all we are the work of Your hand. **Isaiah 64: 8 (NKJV)**

God's transformation of us through the Holy Spirit comes in four ways: breaking, melting, moulding and filling. This is a continuous cycle in our lives as we submit ourselves to Him.

In Jeremiah 18:6, God speaks to the Prophet about Israel. He sends him down to the potter's house, and as Jeremiah watches the potter at work, God speaks to him.

Verse six says, "O house of Israel, can I not do with you as this potter?" says the Lord. "Look as the clay is in the potter's hand, so are you in my hand."

Let's look at a process the potter goes through. He wants to remake a clay pot into something beautiful, perfect and a replica of an image he carries in his mind. He breaks the pot into pieces so he can melt the clay and use it to mould a new pot. Think about it: when we are going through fiery trials, the strain of the situation breaks us. It seems very painful at the time but God simply wants to transform you into His image and likeness. Get excited at the prospect of being transformed daily into the image of God.

Prayer:

Lord, break me! Transform my mind. Make me more like Jesus every day. Amen.

Charge:

Consider it a sheer gift, friends, when tests and challenges come at you from all sides. You know that under pressure your faith-life is forced into the open and shows its true colors. So don't try to get out of anything prematurely. Let it do its work, so you become mature and well developed, not deficient in any way.
James 1:2-4 (MSG)

HIS TRANSFORMATION AGENDA - BREAK

God is the Potter who puts us together. We come broken to pieces but He mends us. This chapter handles two instances of "breaking" in our lives: sin and challenges.

> *But now, O Lord, You are our Father. We are the clay, and You our potter, and all we are the work of Your hand.* **Isaiah 64: 8 (NKJV)**

Sin: Being broken by sin is when we become disobedient to God's way and insist on ours. We get ourselves into situations that are called "breakers". God desires that we obey Him so our lives become secure in Him.

Challenges: Sometimes we become victims of our circumstances – rape, physical abuse, poverty, theft, betrayal, death of a loved one, etc. These experiences shape our outlook of life. Depending on the extent of the damage, the situation can leave us broken and battered, needing the healing touch of our heavenly Father.

Regardless of the situation you are confronted with, the most important thing is to hold on as the Potter puts us back together again. Praise God from whom all good things come.

Prayer:

Thank you Lord for your healing touch in my life. I may be broken but I come to you Lord; You will make me whole again. Life may have fed me bad circumstances, but I rise believing in the power of God to heal and perfect all that concerns me. Thank you, Father, in Jesus' name I pray. Amen.

Charge:

Understand that you are the work of His hands. He wants to put you back together again. Believe this and never become a victim of your circumstance. You are wonderfully and beautifully made by the Potter.

GOD'S WILL

"Don't copy the behaviour and customs of this world, but let God transform you into a new person by changing the way you think. Then you will learn to know God's will for you, which is good and pleasing and perfect."

ROMANS 12:2 (NLT)

THE WAITING GAME – WAIT ON

Over time, I discovered two waiting situations with God. They are what I refer to as "wait on" and "wait for". The difference between the two are the keywords; "on" and "for". To "wait on" connotes a presence while to "wait for" connotes an absence and/or an expectation of an arrival.

Let's look at waiting on something.

But those who wait on the Lord shall renew their strength; they shall mount up with wings like eagles, they shall run and not be weary, they shall walk and not faint. **Isaiah 40:31(NKJV)**

The Holy Spirit provided a very simple illustration to the "wait on" situation. He used an analogy of a restaurant, a guest, a menu and a waiter. In an ideal restaurant, you are handed a menu and a waiter is assigned to handle all your requests.

Now picture this. God is your guest and you are the waiter. The difference here is that the menu is unknown to you (in a place of total submission to His will). So

God makes a request and you serve Him and of course, you MUST give Him a great experience (no fussing, no advising or helping God).

Most times, we equate waiting on God with a period of fasting but the Holy Spirit clarifies that the fasting is a key to understanding God's ideal requests from us. When we fast, we subdue the flesh and allow our spirit connect readily with God's Spirit. This brings us to a place of total submission to His will. God loves a great meal of praise, a delicious serving of worship, an amazing delight of faith-filled prayers, a double whopper of soulful giving and many more on His menu. And of course, He tips us generously with virtues such as strength (Isaiah 40:31, Psalm 27:14), inheritance (Psalm 37:9, 34), His words of encouragement, clarity of vision, joy immeasurable etc.

Prayer:

Father, I thank you today for an opportunity to delight You with answers to your requests! What do you desire? I thank you for grace to abound in all things. Amen!

Charge:

Our attitude of waiting on God has to change from requesting for things from God to letting Him make the requests! Wait on the Lord, ask for His requests and surprise Him with your service. Build strength! Walk! Run! Fly! Soar!

THE WAITING GAME

Strength building in Christ is characterised by waiting periods. Whether we are waiting on God or waiting for Him, it provides an opportunity to deepen our relationship with Him. Let's look at the waiting situation in "wait for".

> *The Lord is good to those who wait for Him, to the soul who seeks Him.* **Lamentations 3:25(NKJV)**

The "wait for" situation connotes an absence and/or an expectation of an arrival, a delivery, a new beginning or divine completion etc. Waiting for God means we expect to see Him come to our help, hear His decision concerning a matter, receive answers to our prayers, or await His manifestations in our lives. First, we must know that God is good to those who wait. It is a two-way street. You trust God during the waiting period and He is good to you during the waiting period. (Psalm 27:13-14)

When we are waiting for God, what should our posture be? Let us look at three key postures:

Hope: A posture that says, "I know and expect You will come no matter when."

Joy: This can be challenging but it is essential when you are waiting for God. Remember that the joy of the Lord is your strength. Joy builds strength for the wait (Psalm 27:14). And yes, it does seem rather challenging waiting joyfully for God to come, especially when faced with a daunting situation.

Faith: An assurance that His perfect will must surely come to pass. This is you knowing that no matter what God allows to happen, it is His ultimate will for you in Christ Jesus. After all, He is a good God. Ever faithful. He knows all you are going through and desires the best outcome for you.

Prayer:

Lord, I am grateful for Your will at work in my life daily. I know You require that I wait for You in this situation. I hope in You Lord, my ever-present help in times of trouble. I know You are coming. I receive strength to wait for You with joy. Amen!

Charge:

As we wait for God, it may tarry, but please don't give up. Hope in God. Don't be discouraged. Let His joy excite you to building faith in Him as you wait for His deliverance. He is coming soon!

SEEKING GOD'S WILL I

Praise the Lord, for His mercies are new every morning. Great is His faithfulness. His love is enduring and He desires we walk with Him every day.

Everything in the world is about to be wrapped up, so take nothing for granted. Stay wide awake in prayers. **1 Peter 4: 7 (MSG)**

Stay alert in the Spirit - pray, fast and inquire of the Lord. I believe strongly that this season will be unique for those who stay close to the Throne Room. God desires a closer walk with us. Let's put off our selfish desires and focus on His needs. In responding to His needs, we draw closer to Him.

In this time, it is very critical for us to be honest about how we have lived our lives so far and compare it to how God expects us to live. It is also a time we need to be very honest about our desires and ask God to align our desires to His will. This is a time to settle down and inquire of God's agenda for your city, state, country and

continent and give of yourself to this agenda. In this time, reflect on your relationship with God, reflect on your relationship with your family, your friends, your colleagues and your business associates. In doing so you will find instructions on how the Lord wants you to operate within these relationships.

As you carry on with your life, don't be discouraged by the things that have not yet happened in your life. Rather set your gaze on Him who is able to direct your path and show you the way to go. It is important in such moments to find time to pray, fast, and listen to what God is saying.

Prayer:

Lord help me seek your face concerning my life. Help me reflect on the past and on the things I could do better today.

Charge:

Spend time praying, fasting and seeking God about His agenda for your life. Ask Him for grace to be aligned to His will.

SEEKING GOD'S WILL II

Praise be to God from whom all good gifts flow. He is truly an amazing God. Ever loving, ever forgiving, ever giving! Isn't the knowledge of that just too beautiful for words? You are charged to stay in position or get in position. It is time for an outpouring of God's Spirit on all flesh! God is seeking those interested in working hand in hand with Him. It's harvest time and the Lord of the harvest is eager for workers.

Everything in the world is about to be wrapped up, so take nothing for granted. Stay wide awake in prayers. **1 Peter 4: 7 (MSG)**

Staying in position or getting in position is critical to God's agenda in your life. It is important to start to prayerfully inquire of God; ask Him this, what do I need to stay or get into position? What excesses do I have to shed to allow a nimble movement to my destiny? What should my focus be on? What should I be asking God for?

Remember that David the Great King always inquired of God before a battle. It was a vital action to the position and victory of the King. Why are you not concerned about being in the centre of God's will? Remember the will of God is good, pleasing (acceptable) and perfect. Romans 12:2. We need to be in the centre of God's will at all times. It's the best place to be.

Prayer:

Father I desire to be in the center of your will. I believe Your will is good, acceptable and perfect for me. I want to position myself rightly to receive the outpouring of your Spirit. Amen.

Charge:

Continue praying, fasting and seeking God about His agenda for humanity and how you can partake of it.

THE FULLNESS OF TIME[1]

Towards the end of the year, and especially during the Christmas holidays, I deliberately take time to reflect on each month and thank God for His steadfastness, unfailing love, unchanging nature and faithfulness towards me. The Holy Spirit reminds me of prophetic words spoken, prayers said, declarations made, dreams had, visions seen, and hopes and desires nurtured. He also shows me my restlessness and careful consideration of a "possible non-performance" (sometimes with the reason it did not happen). Yes, many of us at some point have to deal with unmet desires. Nevertheless, I am reminded of this phase of my life and it is my utmost desire and prayer that you catch this revelation.

> *Shall I bring to the moment of birth and not cause to bring forth says the Lord? Shall I who causes to bring forth shut the womb? says your God.* **Isaiah 66:9 (AMP)**

1 This topic is treated in five parts which can be found on pages 54, 56, 58, 114 and 116

Has God spoken things to you and you are left wondering how they will come to pass? Let's look at the birth of John the Baptist. When his birth was announced to his father, it seemed far-fetched, so much so that Zechariah asked for a sign out of unbelief. However, consider the words of Angel Gabriel as he spoke of the birth in Luke 1:13. Do not be afraid for your prayer is heard (paraphrased). From my study Bible, the word heard as used in Greek language implied that it (the need) was no longer prayed for because they (Zechariah and Elizabeth) were getting old. However, when it was time for the prophecy to come to pass, John was born.

God's words are potent – full of life and power. Whether He has spoken directly to you or through another, His Word is out there, and He will perform all that He has said. Nevertheless, we must ensure our understanding works with His timing. I believe there is an appointed time for prophesies, dreams, purposes, visions etc. There will be a moment of birth and a safe delivery of all things spoken by God and His prophets over His people. The vision is for an appointed time. What is your stance in the Spirit? Are you excited?

If you are still counting the losses of the past, this message is for you. Re-align yourself to what God is saying about you and your purpose. Remind yourself of what He has spoken about concerning you. Take in His Word. Get pregnant with expectation. The time of birthing is near.

Prayer:

God, enlighten my spirit man. I need a revelation of the birthing of Your word today in my life. In Jesus' Name I pray. Amen!

Charge:

Get pregnant with a desire for God's purpose. Feed the pregnancy with the daily diet of God's word. Make sure you take your faith vitamins. Drink from the springs of praise and worship and remember to always check in day and night with the doctor, Jesus.

THE FULLNESS OF TIME – THE STANCE OF BELIEF

We continue our study of the different stances to take in the Spirit in preparation for the manifestation of God's promises over our lives.

I have identified four positions to take, though the list is inexhaustive. I will explore these four positions – **belief** (accepting God's word), **sticking to the name He has given you** (tenacity on what He has said), **obedience** (when He gives instructions) and being a **blessing** to others (love and charity).

Belief, in the context of this study, refers to accepting God's spoken word over you.

> *Then Mary said, "Behold the maidservant of the Lord! Let it be to me according to your word." And the angel departed from her.* **Luke 1: 38 (NKJV)**

Mary was very accepting of God's prophecy through the Angel Gabriel. She readily agreed and was verbal in her agreement. Remember in verse 37, Angel Gabriel said

that nothing was impossible with God – giving Elizabeth's pregnancy as an example of how awesome God is at performing His word. Mary quickly latched on to the word and declared, "Be it unto me as you have spoken." God's word is potent, full of life and power. Whether He has spoken directly to you or through another, His Word is out there and He will perform all that He has said. Nevertheless, is your stance that of belief or disbelief? Are you saying to God, "Be it unto me as You have said", or are you just letting things be?

Today, I challenge you to take the stance of belief. Verbally agree with God's word. Be like Mary and declare to God your readiness to be all that He has called you to be.

Prayer:

Father, all that You have spoken concerning me I receive; I accept it eagerly in the name of Jesus. Amen

Charge:

Make a list of every word or prophecy spoken to you. Speak each one out and respond with, "God, I am your bondservant. Let it be to me according to your word." Then watch God perform! Alleluia!

THE FULLNESS OF TIME – STICK TO THE NAME

What a glorious God we have! His mercies are new every morning! It's a great day to be alive. Let no stone praise God in your place. Give Him resounding praise today. He is worthy! As we continue our study of the different stances to have in the Spirit, let's look at sticking to the name God has given us.

So it was, on the eighth day, that they came to circumcise the child; and they would have called him by the name of the father Zacharias. His mother answered and said, 'No; he shall be called John.' **Luke 1:59-60 (NKJV)**

When Elizabeth gave birth, the neighbours desired to name the child after his dad but the mother said no. She stuck to the name Angel Gabriel had given, even when the neighbours insisted otherwise. When they asked Zacharias to name the child, he wrote John!

Two things stood out to me in these verses: Elizabeth

wasn't around when the Angel visited Zacharias – how then did she know the name? The only explanation is that Zacharias must have conveyed it to her. She took this word and trusted the authenticity of it. Secondly, she stuck to that conveyed word and against the neighbours' requests named their son John. I use this story to point to two key things in maintaining tenacious stance as we wait expectantly for the manifestation of God's promises.

- God's word is to be received, trusted and obeyed.
- When circumstances speak contrary to what God has said, resist it, and then speak what God says.

It's time we start being tenacious about God's word or prophetic words spoken to our lives by His servants. We should never allow circumstances or people name us otherwise. If God says He is your Healer, then trust in that word. If He says He has set you on a hill, then believe you are meant to be seen. If he speaks peace and everything around you speaks otherwise, keep speaking God's peace to yourself and your family. What is God saying to you today? Hold on to that word. Watch it come to pass in the fullness of time!

Prayer:

Heavenly Father, I choose your word over every circumstance. I will be all that you have called me to be. In Jesus' name. Amen.

Charge:

Go back and thank God for His word and then hold on to the word tenaciously! Our God is near!

BIRTHING A NEW NATION – A CRY FOR REVIVAL

The world is currently going through a lot of challenges or what could be referred to as birth pains. This is a time to birth new nations fully aligned with God's agenda. Nations enthroned in God's righteousness and ruled by men and women of right standing, united and advancing, progressive and peaceful.

The Holy Spirit made a clear difference between a country and a nation to me. This happened when I went looking for a definition and realised that in declaring God's will, there has to be a focus on using the term **nation** and not **country**. This is very key.

This is another window that has been opened in the spirit realm and we must seize this moment. The time has come for us to enthrone God's agenda in our nation. A **nation** is a large body of people united by a common descent, history, culture or language and inhabiting a particular state or territory while a **country** is a nation with its own government, occupying a particular territory.

This is a day of trouble, of disgrace, when it is time to birth and there is no strength to bring forth. It would be a big shame if we cannot bring forth a new nation under God in this time.
Isaiah 37:3 (paraphrased)

We must push out the baby. It is time to birth and we MUST do so by decrees and declarations. Our destinies are tied to our nations. All we can ever be in God's will for us is right in our country. Since this is so, what steps are you taking to ensure that you are aligned and positioned to be in God's agenda for the new nation?

What are we amplifying? What is the Church amplifying? What is our driving force every morning we get up? What are we declaring daily?

Prayer:

Lord, let your revival come upon this nation. In Jesus' name. Amen.

Charge:

Keep praying for the revival of your nation.

BEING A WITNESS

"You are my witnesses," declares the LORD, "and my servant whom I have chosen, so that you may know and believe me and understand that I am he. Before me no god was formed, nor will there be one after me."

Isaiah 43:10 (NIV)

SPREADING THE JESUS FRAGRANCE

Imagine how you always sense the presence of a loved one once you step into the room through a familiar scent? You instantly know that Mum or Dad have been in that room. Have you ever considered what it will be like to wear a Jesus perfume?

> *But thank God! He has made us His captives and continues to lead us along in Christ's triumphal procession. Now He uses us to spread the knowledge of Christ everywhere, like a sweet perfume. Our lives are a Christ-like fragrance rising up to God.* **2 Corinthians 2:14-15a(NLT)**

In the scripture above, we see that God uses us to spread the knowledge of Christ. This simply means that in every aspect of life, we should bring the fragrance of Christ that promotes the knowledge of our Lord. This fragrance proves to people that you are different, you are reborn, and you are a child of God. You transform places by the power and presence of the Lord Jesus. Your actions advertise the kingdom of God, such that when people

start to say, "I like this fragrance" or ask, "Who are you wearing?" you will simply answer, "I'm wearing Jesus!"

Our lives should give out a sweet aroma of Christ working through us and liberating the lives of others. As we submit every day to the work of the Holy Spirit in our lives, we build our aroma of Christ. When we come in contact with people, they should recognise that which we carry and its saving power unto them that believe.

So, what aroma are you carrying? Are you wearing the Jesus Perfume? Or do you wear a different fragrance? Is your aroma spreading the knowledge of Christ or the knowledge of man? Is this aroma bringing salvation or death to many? Today, consider what aroma you are giving off.

Prayer:

Jesus, I want to be more like you. Help me die to self and live for you. I want to be the Jesus Perfume, spreading Your fragrance in every place so I can bring people to the knowledge of You. Amen.

Charge:

Reflect on the fragrance you are giving off. Ask the Holy Spirit to help with the areas of your life that need improving on. Be that sweet-smelling fragrance that is pleasing to God. Let Him use you to draw souls to Himself.

LIVING YOUR GOD-STORY

We all have a God-story (defined as God's intervention and redefinition of our lives). God desires that we live life according to His script so that we are purposeful in this journey of life.

But the story we're given is a God-story not an Abraham-story. What we read in the scripture is, "Abraham entered into what God was doing for him, and that was the turning point. He trusted God to set him right instead of trying to be right in his own." **Romans 4: 2-3(MSG)**

Romans 4 considers our father of faith, Abraham, and God's awesome intervention in his life. The Message Translation of the Bible provides clarity of God's word and how Abraham held on to it without wavering despite the circumstances. Picture this: Abraham is going about life normally, writing his story and suddenly, God takes an interest and decides to rewrite his story to a God-story. He calls him "father" (though he had no offspring). He

calls him out of his comfort zone into a journey of faith, trust and obedience.

The word says, "Abraham trusted God to fulfill His promise to him without wavering or tiptoeing around God's promise and asking skeptical questions. He plunged right into the promise and came up strong, ready for God, sure that God would make good on what he said." **Romans 4: 19-25(MSG)**

So, what has God said concerning you? What has He called you to do? What is He calling you out of and into? What is your God-story? Have you plunged right in or have you remained undecided because of the "realities" staring you in the face? I urge you today, get in there and hold on. Let go and let God! Trust Him to perform and watch Him be God!

Prayer:

Heavenly Father, I choose to be obedient to Your Word. Today, I embrace my God-story and I am eager to walk with you Lord. Amen!

Charge:

Start living your God-story today. Do not fear! Once God has said it, He will do it. Play your own part by trusting Him and believing His word concerning you.

BEING BOLD AND DELIBERATE

God expects us to wake up every day focused on the decisions we have made in line with His will. He wants us to be more deliberate and particular about the things we do. He wants to trust our judgements and actions in life. This deliberateness comes through boldness. When we know what we have, we will be more particular in seeing them manifest. We should not act like slaves while we are sons. Slaves beg their way through, but sons demand what is theirs.

And the Lord looked upon him, and said, "Go in this thy might, and thou shalt save Israel from the hand of the Midianites: have not I sent thee?" **Judges 6:14 (KJV)**

The strength of the enemy is in our ignorance. When we know who and whose we are, we go through life with clarity of vision. We will also pursue the mandates God called us into. Our knowledge is based on revelation and it comes through constant relationship with God. Gideon had a walk with God and he was able to fulfil purpose.

How was it possible that Noah believed God to have built an ark even at a time when rain had not yet visited the earth? The answer lies in his relationship with God. Also, Abraham had a deep walk with God so much so that he could believe God to raise Isaac from the dead if he killed him. Abraham did not tell anyone what God told him, not even Sarah. He kept it to himself and ran along. As we walk with God, we realise that it's not every one of God's instruction that should be shared because if we do, people will talk us out of it.

When we have a deep relationship with God, we become fully persuaded and no one can dissuade us from achieving our desires.

God is always emphasising the need for us to march with boldness into greater territories and unknown grounds in victory. In the area of our finance, we should boldly cash in from Jesus' bank account.

Prayer:

Father, I receive the grace to grow deeper in God, and to receive fresh boldness to march into greater places and territories. I take authority over every negative force in my life. In Jesus' name. Amen.

Charge:

Be bold, be strong, for the Lord your God is with you.

THE PEACEMAKERS

There is a lot of turmoil in our present world. Wars and rumours of wars, refugee crises, natural disasters, communities killing each over land disputes, racism at its height in nations, animosity, suicide, bitterness and hate – the list of death and dying goes on. In Nigeria, a young man frustrated with the tough life set himself ablaze in the city of Lagos. These are dire times. Many people are angry and rightly so. However, the Spirit of God has this to say to us in these dark times:

Blessed are the peacemakers, for they shall be called children of God. **Matthew 5:9 (NIV)**

God's call to us in this time is to represent Him as peacemakers. That is our identity in Him. The Message translation says, "You're blessed when you can show people how to cooperate instead of competing or fighting. That's when you discover who you really are, and your place in God's family."

Our Father in Heaven instructs us through His word, to preach and pray for peace to a hurting world. Rather than preach violence or disorder, God says, "Teach them to cooperate. Teach them My love. Teach them My

peace. Share My Joy with everyone. Give of yourself and your resources. Help your leaders to make things right."

I know this is tough especially if you have lost loved ones to these very unfortunate circumstances, however, the teaching of Christ turns the worldview on its head. In Luke 6:27-30, He says, "To you who are ready for the truth, I say this: love your enemies. Let them bring out the best in you, not the worst. When someone gives you a hard time, respond with the energies of prayer for that person. If someone slaps you in the face, stand there and take it. If someone grabs your shirt, gift-wrap your best coat and make a present of it. If someone takes unfair advantage of you, use the occasion to practice the servant life. No more tit-for-tat stuff. Live generously." (**MSG**) Selah!

Today, let's represent our Father to the world, being the peacemakers He has called us to be as His sons and daughters. His grace is sufficient. He is with you always.

Prayer:

Father, today, I choose to be a peacemaker to the hurting world. Touch my lips with your grace. Holy Spirit fill me to overflow that I may be a blessing everywhere I tread.

Charge:

Make peace not war.

WORSHIP

"Give unto the Lord, O ye mighty, give unto the Lord glory and strength.

Give unto the Lord the glory due unto his name; worship the Lord in the beauty of holiness."

PSALM 29:1-2 (KJV)

NO QUICK FIX – BECOME A TRUE WORSHIPPER

We were created to worship our Lord. God loves our worship so much that He inhabits our praises. To inhabit is to *live in*, to *dwell within*. When your worship rises up to God, He steps down into your space. What a wonderful thing! God comes to dwell in your life, your home, everywhere you lift up a song; He listens. You can converse with Him, fellowship with Him, sing love songs to Him and just celebrate Him. When last did you give God awesome worship?

> *But the hour is coming, and now is, when the true worshipers will worship the Father in spirit and truth; for the Father is seeking such to worship Him.* **John 4: 23 (NKJV)**

We live in hard and perilous times! There is so much going on and so much to do. Church has become a quick fix mechanism for us so much so that many show up every Sunday to get help for the week, and truth be told, the fix lasts only till Sunday evening, then we are back to ground

zero. Solution: we need to be filled continually with the Spirit of God. We have to come back to a place of true worship to our God! We sing to Him but our hearts are far away, thinking about the next deal, our mistakes and our worries. Our lips say the right words but our hearts are dipped in disbelief.

God knows all about your problems. Remember, He is the way-maker. He has sorted you out. So when you come to him daily, focus on Him and not your issues. Love Him with all you've got and celebrate your deliverer. Worship Him in spirit and in truth.

Prayer:

I'm coming back to the heart of worship where it's all about You, Jesus. I set my eyes on You and You alone.

Charge:

It's who you are and the way you live that counts before God. Your worship must engage your spirit in the pursuit of truth. Those are the kind of people the Father is looking for, those who are simply and honestly themselves before Him in their worship. *God is a Spirit and those who worship him must do it out of their very being, with their spirits, their true selves, in adoration.* **John 4:23-24 (MSG)**

TO WORSHIP HIM

When you follow the story of our creation and the reason for our being, you will realise that we are truly special and precious to God. God created us to have constant fellowship with Him. We were made to worship God. He deserves all of our worship and praise. We are His creation and made in His image and likeness. Even with the fall of Adam, God devised a plan that will forever close the separation caused by the sin of Adam.

> *Therefore, I urge you, brothers and sisters, in view of God's mercy, to offer your bodies as a living sacrifice, holy and pleasing to God. This is your true and proper worship.* **Romans 12:1**

Worship is about reverence and adoration of our Father. To revere God is to have deep respect for or admire Him as your heavenly Father. To adore God is to love, cherish and appreciate Him. The text above refers to a reverence of Him in our bodies which are His temple. When we adore God through praise and worship, He dwells within

us in our spirits, nurturing and grooming us to be more like Him. God cannot share His space with another. He is a jealous God and desires that your affections are for Him and Him alone.

Whatever is harmful to the body does not have a place in our lives as our bodies are the temple of God. We are the new Holy of Holies and so must, by His Spirit, live holy lives. This is our true worship to God. As we worship God in singing of psalms and songs of praise, let our bodies also worship Him.

God gets pleasure out of us. He inhabits our praises (Psalm 22:3). He delights over us with singing!

Prayer:

Dear Father, I love that You delight in me and that You rejoice over me with singing. Holy Spirit, help me present my body to the Father as a sweet-smelling sacrifice.

Charge:

You were made to worship the Lord God Almighty. Speak good of God. Tell people of His goodness. This is also a form of worship.

GRACE

For the grace of God has appeared that offers salvation to all people. It teaches us to say "No" to ungodliness and worldly passions, and to live self-controlled, upright and godly lives in this present age.

TITUS 2:11-12 (NIV)

GRACE IN TIME OF NEED

Our relationship with the Father is one born out of grace. By grace, we are saved and ushered into the Kingdom of Light. By grace, Christ birthed our redemption through His death on the Cross.

Grace is help from above. Grace is available in our time of need.

> *Let us then approach God's throne of grace with confidence, so that we may receive mercy and find grace to help us in our time of need.* **Hebrews 4:16**

By Christ's death and resurrection, the separation of man from God has been completely taken away. And so we have this confidence, that if God be for us, who can be against us? This is an assurance of our belonging to the family of light.

The text says we should approach God's throne of grace with confidence. God's grace is ours for the asking. When we face diverse trials and temptations, when we feel like we can't go on, when life seems dreary and for-

lorn, that's the time to lean on His grace to get help and deliverance.

Grace is unmerited favour from God. We are underserving, yet He desires to give us grace.

It has been made available and we have been invited to approach God with confidence. We are assured of His grace in our time of need. Alleluia.

Prayer:

Dear Father, give me grace and strength to face all the issues of life I may encounter today.

Charge:

Receive grace in your time of need. Ask the Father. It is made available.

IN HIS TIME

Thankful for His mercies and the opportunity to keep at the purpose journey daily, we look at the beauty of God's timing. Yes, the beauty of God's timing despite the ugliness of life sometimes.

He has made everything beautiful in its time. **Ecclesiastes 3:11a (NKJV)**

Our lives are made up of times and seasons. Time was created by God though He lives in eternity. We live and operate in time, and everything happens or comes to us in God's time and designated season. Waiting on God's timing is very challenging; in fact, it seems really difficult. Whenever we question God's timing, it is often because we are looking for guidance or deliverance from a difficult situation. But the good news is that God is never late. Our God requires that we go through different stages so we can mature. When we know this, our waiting becomes light. We start to focus more on trusting God

and patiently waiting on Him, knowing that He controls the times and seasons of our lives.

God makes all things beautiful in His time. He is our Father whose priority is to ensure we live a life worthy of His calling. When we understand that He is driven by love, we will know that His perfect timing of things is to our advantage. Going ahead of Him puts us at a disadvantage and makes us a prey to the enemy.

Today, have faith in God's timing. It may seem like it's never going to happen but be assured that waiting is God's good and perfect will. His grace has been made available to aid our waiting period.

Prayer:

Thank You, blessed Father for the grace to wait. Your timing is perfect and I trust in You!

Charge:

Understand that God's timing is the best for you. Take delight in the Lord, and He will give you the desires of your heart. **Psalm 37:4**

BE KIND TO THE POOR

As we strive to grow daily in God through His Holy Spirit, we uncover more truths as we dig deeper into our relationship with Him. Giving of yourself and your substance is key to spreading God's love through heartfelt actions in our homes, offices, businesses and community. We are God's love representatives and must show His goodness to others by being like Him.

Whoever is kind to the poor lends to the LORD, and He will reward them for what they have done. **Proverbs 19:17(NIV)**

God cares deeply about the poor. Giving is an act of love as demonstrated by God through Christ. We often hear that God can't owe anyone. However, our text today shows an exception to the rule. This is because of the importance of this group to God. Christ said during his ministry that the poor (in spirit and in flesh) would always be among us. We see in these times that help is needed in almost every corner. What acts of love and kindness are you spreading in your environment? Do

you turn up your nose at the poor and become unconcerned about their well-being? Do you call law enforcement officers on the poor because they are trespassing or overstepping set boundaries? Many have fallen on hard times and the poor are getting the hardest part of it. Jobs, education, health, feeding and housing are becoming more and more alien to most people. The wealth gap is widening daily. Wars have separated families, creating internal and external refuges within countries. How do we show God's love to those in need around us?

Today, God says to you, "Lend to me by being kind, giving, supporting and honouring these ones and I will repay." Don't be limited by your resources. Collaborative actions with others can go a long way to alleviate some of the suffering around us. You can do more. Be God's friend today. Lend to Him. Give to the poor.

Prayer:

Dear Father, I thank you for the opportunity to enlighten my spirit with the act of giving. I will be a blessing to my world through the work you have committed to my hands.

Charge:

Give generously to them and do so without a grudging heart; then, because of this, the LORD your God will bless you in all your works and in everything you put your hand to do. **Deuteronomy 15:10 (NIV)**

PRAISE AND THANKSGIVING

"Enter with the password, "Thank you!"
Make yourselves at home talking praise.
Thank him. Worship him."

PSALM 100:4 (MESSAGE TRANSLATION)

THE DAY GIFT

The steadfast love of our God never ceases, His mercies never come to an end, they are new every morning, great is your faithfulness oh Lord! – *Hillsong Worship*

> *This is the day the Lord has made, we will rejoice and be glad in it.* **Psalm 118:24(NKJV)**

I go walking every other day in the week and on those days, I have noticed that every morning has its own look and feel. The Holy Spirit pointed this out to me. He made me realise how different each day is, full of its own promises and possibilities. A new dawn, a new rising, a jolly new day! Imagine a package you were not expecting is delivered to you from a loved one. You eagerly tear open the wrapping paper, excited at what may be in the box. Every day is a gift given to us by God, the creator of all things. Our breath is not ours to have. If you are awake in the morning, it is not of your own doing.

How do you embrace the gift of each day – with a

sour attitude or with delight? Do you, with great expectation, unwrap your day knowing that it holds the great promises of God? Or do you wish that the sun didn't rise? Do you grudgingly welcome the day or do you exclaim with joy and praise at the possibilities of every new day? Do you say a big thank you to the giver of the day or do you simply ignore Him? God wishes for us to know that every day is new and is His DAILY loving gift to us as a Father. Psalm 118: 24 reminds us that the day is made by Him. The psalmist declares that we rejoice and are glad in it. So welcome your day differently; it matters to God. Embrace the gift of each day with both hands and unwrap it with joy. Rejoice at the dawning of a new day. It is a privilege.

Prayer:

Thank you Lord for a brand new day. I am excited at what today holds in store for me. I am expectant at what you have prepared for me today and take hold of this. I will not waste today. In Jesus' name I pray. Amen.

Charge:

Enter with the password "Thank you!" Make yourselves at home, talking praise. Thank Him. Worship Him. **Psalm 100:4 – (MSG)**

THE MIDNIGHT HOUR

I have often wondered about the concept of midnight prayers. I figured it must have come out of the Paul and Silas experience, with the ground-shaking miracle of their release from the maximum-security cell in the jailhouse.

> *Along about midnight, Paul and Silas were at prayer and singing a robust hymn to God. The other prisoners couldn't believe their ears. Then, without warning, a huge earthquake! The jailhouse tottered, every door flew open, all the prisoners were loose.* **Acts 16: 25 -26 (MSG)**

The miracle from this passage happened at midnight. Paul and Silas had been in jail, badly beaten and under guard. Do you think they just started praying at midnight or way before then? I strongly believe they started praying and singing way before midnight, if not for anything, to encourage each other. As they gathered strength from weak bodies and soared in the spirit, rendering praises to God, a miracle happened at MIDNIGHT! Let's understand

that the midnight analogy is not really about a particular praying time but about the power of God to turn a situation around. It's the spiritual timing of God's intervention on our behalf because of our praise, prayers, supplication and most importantly, His mercies. The best part is, other people get liberated alongside us like we saw in the ground-shaking miracle of Paul and Silas! (vs 26)

Let's repent of the things created out of misinterpretation and focus on what God expects from us in the midst of our trials and tribulations. Let's begin way before ***the midnight hour*** to pray and praise God and look forward to that earth-shaking, groundbreaking miracle at MIDNIGHT! Simply put, praying at midnight changes nothing. Trusting and praising God in the midst of trials and tribulations creates a change and brings about deliverance.

Prayer:

Lord, You are my deliverer and ever-present help in time of trouble. I set my gaze on You and You alone. I choose today to praise You in the midst of my challenges and trials.

Charge:

Pray and praise your way out of every limiting factor, every trial and every tribulation! He is our deliverer. Late in the midnight hour, He will surely turn it around!

THIS IS THE YEAR OF GOD AND YOU I

In my life, I have deliberately adopted a lifestyle of thanksgiving. The heart of gratitude ***expresses*** and ***communicates*** immense appreciation to God. Thanksgiving to God is like building a memorial that glorifies His holy name and displays to others His immense power in all of the earth and in your life. I chose to build deeper levels of my relationship with God, and I am committed to partnership with Him on the journey of life. That song that says "there is no place I'll rather be than in Your Presence" is my anchor song.

What have you anchored your life on so far? What is your go-to fix? I am anchored on God's Word! This year, I choose to believe His word. There are seven anchors I hold firmly in my heart and I will share the first three with you in this chapter. I pray that you find stability and security in His Word:

My Stance: *It is good to give thanks to the Lord, and to sing praises to Your Name, O Most High…* **Psalms 92:1 (NKJV)**

I have chosen to be thankful. (So help me God!) No matter what, my entire countenance will always be thankful. I will count my blessings daily. I will be thankful to God, friends, foes, family etc. God's got my back! He's for me, in me and with me. Enter His gates with thanksgiving and His courts with praise!

My Position/Placing: *You have caused men to ride over our heads; we went through fire and through water but You brought us out to rich fulfillment.* **Psalms 66:12 (NKJV)**

Other versions use the following words: abundance, wealthy place, a large place, place of safety, a well-watered place, or a place of plenty. Sometime in the past, the economy was in recession and businesses had taken a really bad blow. Yet, all those trials and tough times have ushered us into a well-watered place and a place of fulfillment. No matter what you think, God has brought you to a wealthy place. Be anchored on this word as where you have been placed this year.

My View of God: *Who* is *like You, O Lord, among the gods? Who is like You, glorious in holiness, fearful in praises, doing wonders?* **Exodus 15:11 (NKJV)**

What is your view of God? Magnify your view with this song sung by the Israelites when they crossed the Red Sea. My view of God? A WONDER WORKING GOD.

Prayer:

Father, today, I choose to believe You and Your Word.

Charge:

It is not too late to write up your Word anchors. Put them up where you can see them daily. The Word works. Alleluia!

THIS IS THE YEAR OF GOD AND YOU II

You are embracing a deeper walk with Him. You are saying to God, *You are all I want and have.* This year, we need to go deeper, dig in and enjoy a robust walk with our Creator. We continue our talk on the yearly anchors. In the first part, we looked at three scriptural anchors; let's look at the remaining four.

My Revelation: *To them God willed to make known what are the riches of the glory of this mystery among the Gentiles: which is Christ in you, the hope of glory.* **Colossians 1:27 (NKJV)**

This word gives me a view of eternity. Christ in Me! My Hope of Glory! It reminds me everything here is temporary. It prods me to focus on eternity and our reign with Christ (my future). It assures me that there is an eternal plan that supersedes that of men. I therefore need to set my entire gaze on Jesus and let Him take the lead in all things. This year, focus on things above (eternal things).

My Heart Stay: *For this reason I also suffer these things; nevertheless I am not ashamed, for I know whom I have believed and am persuaded that He is able to keep what I have committed to Him until that Day.* **2 Timothy 1:12 (NKJV)**

This is my doubt breaker. My confidence in God should be completely unshakeable and this scripture helps me. I know that God is responsible for and towards me.

My Mantra: *I know that You can do everything, and that no purpose of Yours can be withheld from You.* **Job 42:2 (NKJV)**

God's purpose for me can never be thwarted! I just need to be in the center of His will. He can do everything! The possibilities in that single statement are limitless. So quit shouting at your enemies and start chanting! Everything will fall into place by His Spirit.

My Charge: *See then that you walk circumspectly, not as fools but as wise.* **Ephesians 5:15 (NKJV)**

Circumspectly *means to be careful and discreet, to be prudent and cautious.* The wisdom of God will pave my way and provide direction. The times are evil and we must be accountable to ourselves and the Holy Spirit in all we do. We must walk carefully, be discreet, prudent and cautious, leaning completely on the wisdom of God.

Prayer:

Father, today, I choose to believe You and Your Word.

Charge:

Write up your Word anchors for your life. Put them up where you can see them daily. The Word works! Alleluia!

THE POWER OF THANKSGIVING

Have you ever set a goal for yourself? Or have you looked back and thought that you were behind in some of the things you desired? You may also be thinking that these things may never happen and find yourself feeling sad about this. I encourage you today: Give thanks. Praise God from whom all good gifts come. Do not be dismayed. He is able.

> *In everything give thanks: for this is the will of God in Christ Jesus concerning you.* **I Thessalonians 5:18 (KJV)**

God commands us to give thanks in everything. He does this because he understands that "a cheerful disposition is good for my health" **(Prov 17:22).** God knows worrying about circumstances or things will only create unpleasant health issues or concerns. He expects us to trust in Him and not waver in our belief that He is God over everything.

Remember, amidst the troubles, there is always something to be thankful about. Being alive is one.

Why is thanksgiving so vital for you?

- It creates a progressive path in God's kingdom for you. Your expectation creates your miracles.
- It positively affects your mental faculty and improves your reasoning. You see things clearly and through the eyes of God.
- It affects the glory of the individual. Praise can return your lost glory.
- Thanksgiving can attract honour and brightness to you.
- It can cause those designed to favour you to remember you.
- Thanksgiving ushers you into God's presence. It is the protocol needed to access God. Come in through the gates with thanksgiving and into His courts with praise.

Prayer:

Today and always, Lord, I praise you in all things. Help me to do this in the name of our Lord Jesus.

Charge:

Today, start a thanksgiving journal. Everyday write down what you are grateful for. Please God with a heart full of praise and thanksgiving. It is for your good.

MAGNIFY GOD

What a beautiful day to be in the presence of the Lord. Every new day excites me because of its possibilities; each new day is created by God and with God all things are possible. How awe-inspiring! Today, I want to let you into a secret that can help us take the limits off God. It's all about magnifying Him.

> *Oh magnify the Lord with me, and let us exalt His name together.* **Psalm 34: 3 (NKJV)**

Magnify, as defined by the dictionary means "to make (something) larger than it is." It also means to praise highly, glorify and to make something bigger, whether in size or in significance. Taking the limits off God means that we need to view Him as bigger than what we see or imagine. We need to see Him in a magnified way. When we see God through our natural human eyes, we tend to see Him smaller than He is, but PRAISE serves as the magnifying lens that makes you see God bigger than

what you perceive. Praise enlarges our view of God. Yes it does!

Take the limits off God, magnify Him through praise. In doing so, you will see the bigness of our God. You will see every impossible thing become possible. You will see every mountain brought low and every valley raised. You will see springs in the deserts. You will see victory in every battle, a way where there seems to be no way, the hand of God on every situation and, most importantly, the unfailing love of God our Father that keeps us.

Prayer:

I praise you, O Lord. Great and mighty are the works of Your hand, from the rising of the sun to the place it sets, Lord, I will praise Your name for evermore. You are highly exalted over all the nations. Your glory rises above the heavens. You are worthy of all praise and honour. Be magnified now and forever.

Charge:

Read the book of Job, chapters 38 – 40

POWER AND AUTHORITY

"Then Jesus came to them and said, "All authority in heaven and on earth has been given to me."

MATTHEW 28:18 (NIV)

OUR VICTORY – SIGNED, SEALED AND DELIVERED

God loves us without fail. This was very clear when He sent the Lord Jesus to reconcile humanity back to God through His death on the Cross. He did not withhold His only son but sent Him to die for us so that we may have eternal life in Him. Amazing love! God ***signed*** off on the death of His only son so that He (God) can have a chance at loving us without restrictions. We can enter in to His presence and not be consumed by His holiness. Alleluia!

> *In Messiah, in Christ, God leads us from place to place in one perpetual victory parade.* **2 Corinthians 2: 14(MSG)**

The text above explains what great benefits we have as children of God through the death of Jesus Christ on the Cross. Accepting Jesus as our Saviour opens us to an awesome relationship with our Father. We have victory over sin and death. Colossians 2: 15 says that "God disarmed the principalities and powers that were raging against us

and made a bold display and public example of them, in triumphing over them in Him and in it (the Cross)."

In Christ we have the VICTORY! This is possible because God made the first and only move needed: He sent Jesus to die for us, to be the holy sacrifice needed for forgiveness of sins.

God is leading us from place to place, trial to trial in one perpetual victory parade! See anew today that you are victorious over all things through Christ our Lord. Alleluia! If you are yet to know and love Jesus, please let Him in. He says, "Look at me. I stand at the door. I knock. If you hear me call and open the door, I'll come right in and sit down to supper with you. Conquerors will sit alongside me at the head table, just as I, having conquered, took the place of honour at the side of my Father. That's my gift to the conquerors!" **Rev. 3: 20 - 21 (MSG)**

Prayer:

Lord Jesus, today, I believe that You died and rose again to give me victory over sin and death. I thank you for being obedient to the Father and reconciling me to Him. Come live in me today and always. Amen.

Charge:

Declare these words: I am more than a conqueror through Christ Jesus. I am victorious in Christ. I can do all things through Christ who strengthens me. In Christ alone, my hope is found. Alleluia!

WHERE ARE YOU SEATED?

If you have ever travelled on a plane or a bus or been transported between cities, you are required to show your ticket or your boarding pass before you are seated. Most times, especially for air travel, your boarding pass must have a seat number.

Recently, I was wondering about a nagging situation and the Holy Spirit asked me: Where are you seated? And then He led me to these scriptures:

"Which He worked in Christ when He raised Him from the dead and seated Him at His right hand in heavenly places, far above all principality and power and might and dominion, and every name that is named, not only in this age but also in that which is to come." **Ephesians 1: 20-21(NKJV)**

". . .and raised us up together, and made us sit together in heavenly places in Christ Jesus." **Ephesians 2: 6(NKJV)**

The scriptures above show where we are seated – in heavenly places with Christ Jesus. I suddenly realised the

Holy Spirit was giving me a lesson on Spiritual Authority and a remembrance of my spiritual ranking. I am seated with Christ by the right hand of the Father far above every situation, so why was I allowing that nagging situation unsettle me? The key challenge then as a believer is the realisation of who you are in Christ, and then exercising your authority. How often do we view things through the natural and let them affect our thoughts and spiritual authority?

Are you seated down here in the natural where all you see are the problems, or are you seated with Christ in Heavenly places? Today, be convinced that you are seated with Christ in heavenly places above all power, principality, might, dominion and every named name. DO NOT FEAR! Speak to every situation! You have the backing of the Father; you can just lean over and speak to Him. You are standing RIGHT by Him. Isn't that such wonderful knowledge? There is a calmness that comes from this knowledge.

Prayer:

Father, please give me a deeper understanding and clarity of my spiritual ranking in You through Jesus Christ. Amen.

Charge:

Declare these words: I am seated with Christ at the right hand of the Father. Through Him I have authority over all things. I am seated in Christ far above all power, principality, might, dominion and every name that is named in this age and in the age to come. I am not afraid! Let Psalm 27:1 be your mantra.

WHY ARE WE NOT ASKING?

The word of God says, "all things are possible to them that believe." How often do you ask God for the impossible? What limits have you set in your asking? Take the limits off and push to expand your territory.

> *Ask of Me and I will give you the nations for your inheritance, and the ends of the earth for your possession.* **Psalm 2:8 (NKJV)**

Very often, we unconsciously become mediocre in our thinking and this ultimately affects what we ask of God. Our petitions start from a place of thought. If you stretch your imagination, you will ask the impossible from God. God says to ask him for the nations. How many business people are looking at expanding their businesses beyond their current cities? How many career persons or professionals are thinking of moving beyond nations or taking their services to nations? How come we are comfortable with where we are when God has given us the charge to ask of Him?

In Psalm 24:1, we are told, "The earth is the Lord's, and all its fullness, the world and those who dwell therein." God created all things. There is nothing He cannot do. Start today to ask of God. Start today to imagine the impossible. Stretch your imagination. When elevated in your place of work or you experience increase in your business, don't allow mediocrity set in. Ask yourself, "God, what more can I do?"

Prayer:

Dear God, expand my mind. I refuse to be mediocre in my thinking. I refuse to be driven by mediocrity in my business, life and ministry. All I ask is that you expand my territory. In Jesus' name. Amen.

Charge:

Say the prayer of Jabez. "Oh, that You would bless me indeed and enlarge my territory, that Your hand would be with me, and that You would keep me from evil…"
1 Chronicles 4:9-10 (NKJV)

HIS POWER AT WORK IN US

Alleluia for our Lord God, Omnipotent reigns! What a delight to know God in these times. He is always ensuring that we remain victorious in every situation. Trusting God and understanding the power at work in us remains key to living a victorious life in Jesus Christ.

> *Now to Him who is able to do exceedingly abundantly above all that we ask or think, according to the power that works in us.* **Ephesians 3:20 (NKJV)**

Ephesians 1: 19- 20 speaks on the working of this mighty power that raised Christ from the dead and seated Him at the right hand of the Father. That is the power at work in you—The Holy Spirit. This same power worked all miracles seen in the Bible: the parting of the Red Sea, the plagues, the healing miracles, raising of the dead etc. How powerful! That's the power at work in us!

Do you know just how powerful God has made you? His word says He has not given us a spirit of fear but of *power*, *love* and a *sound mind*. From the very beginning,

God has equipped us with power to achieve and shine. We are not to give in to fear, but rather, we are to tap into the power at work in us and stay victorious in the face of challenges.

However, His power in us remains a potential until we put it in action. How do we transform from just potential to action? Three simple things: **praying, studying the word and speaking the word**! Praying builds an intimate relationship with the Father and your faith in Him. Studying reveals the God-story and your role. Speaking the word reveals your trust in God and your eagerness to see His promises at work.

God wants you to succeed and He has equipped you with all that you need. Tap into the power today. Build on it and see God work great things in your life!

Prayer:

Father, please give me the spirit of wisdom and revelation to build my knowledge of You. Grant that the eyes of my understanding be enlightened that I may know the working of Your mighty power in and through me. In Jesus' name. Amen.

Charge:

Put the power of God at work in you to good use. Set it in motion this week and watch God work through you to impact the lives of people.

SPEAKING DELIBERATELY – EVERY WORD SPOKEN COUNTS

Take a moment and think: What words have you spoken today? Do you know that every idle word spoken will be judged? God listens to every single word uttered by us and He weighs each one. Do you speak with deliberate words or do you speak carelessly? We must learn to speak deliberately to everything; whether it is to persons, situations, or to God. Jesus Christ was very clear about idle words.

> *But I say to you that for every idle word men may speak, they will give account of it in the day of judgment. For by your words you will be justified, and by your words you will be condemned.* **Matthew 12: 36-37(NKJV)**

By your words, you are justified or condemned! That is deep. We need to be careful with words. The Bible, in the book of James, is very clear on how destructive the tongue can be. James is very apt in his advice: "Be slow to anger, slow to speak and quick to listen." A popular idiom

says we have two ears and one mouth, because we are meant to listen twice as hard! When God was creating, He spoke. So therefore, our words must be deliberate. What are you saying about your family, friends, business, work and ministry? Idle words or deliberate words? Our words are powerful when spoken into the atmosphere. Weigh your words before you utter them. Speak life to everyone. Be deliberate, speak words that are meaningful and laced with grace. Bless, don't curse; yes, even to those who hate and use you. It is the "God way." Speak life to yourself, create your day. Be victorious in the face of adversity. David won the war of words with Goliath before the actual battle began. Read that story again. Say what you mean and mean what you say! May God help us as we learn and re-learn the concept of speaking life!

Prayer:

Today, Lord, help me speak careful words. Amen.

Charge:

Do not curse the King, even in your thought; do not curse the rich, even in your bedroom; for a bird of the air may carry your voice, and a bird in flight may tell the matter. **Ecclesiastes 10: 20 (NKJV)**

Speak deliberate words.

THE FULLNESS OF TIME – OBEDIENCE

Bless the Lord, oh my soul, and forget not all His benefits! **Psalm 103:2 (NKJV)**. Regardless of what you are going through, bless the Lord all the same. Remember we are being tenacious about His Word. As we continue our study of the different stances to have in the Spirit in preparation for the manifestation of God's word, I will like to introduce the importance of obedience.

> *If you are willing and obedient, you shall eat the good of the land.* **Isaiah 1:19 (NKJV)**

When expectant and waiting for the fullness of time (God's fulfilment of a spoken word), obedience is paramount to getting there. God treasures obedience. It means you trust Him completely to follow through with what He has asked you to do. Consider the story of Mary. Her fiancé, Joseph, was obedient to God by not sending her away. Rather, he believed God's messenger knowing

that she was carrying the Christ. So, once we accept the word (**Luke 2:38**), the next step will be to obey it.

Samuel the Prophet wrote that it's better to obey than to offer sacrifice. Sometimes what could be holding your breakthrough could be disobedience to God's word. Who or what are you unforgiving of? What is causing so much bitterness in your heart that it has swallowed up the Word? What has God asked you for that you are withholding? What has He asked you to put on the altar (your Isaac) that you have hidden? Who or what has He asked you to bless? What relationships has He asked you to let go of? What great leap of faith has He expected of you and you still hide in the shadows? What level of impatience with God has created a high level of disobedience to His word in your life? Today, my loved ones, let us all REPENT! Yes, let's get back to the basics and come to God with childlike adoration and complete trust!

Prayer:

Father, today I repent of every act of disobedience. Holy Spirit, please help me obey God completely. In Jesus' name. Amen.

Charge:

Reflect on Psalm 139:23-24. Strive to obey God. Listen to His instructions. I pray grace on you to stand up and be counted for Jesus!

THE FULLNESS OF TIME – LOVE AND CHARITY

In this final session in the series – The Fullness of Time – I want to teach on love and charity (giving) because they are the true nature of our Heavenly Father. "For God so loved the world that He gave His only Son." The action of love is to give.

> *But for right now, until that completeness, we have three things to do to lead us toward that consummation: Trust steadily in God, hope unswervingly, love extravagantly and the best of the three is love.* **1 Corinthians 13: 13 (MSG)**

And remember the words of the Lord Jesus, that He said, "It is more blessed to give than *to receive.*" **Acts 20:35b (NKJV)**

Extravagance is defined as going beyond the bounds of reason through your actions, demands, opinions or passion. It is also defined as going beyond what is deserved or justifiable. This clarifies exactly how

God expects us to love. If you know God and you are in Him, you will love like Him – going beyond what is expected of you. Surprise people pleasantly with the love you show them. Yes! While waiting for that breakthrough, love, give, nurture and encourage others. Love extravagantly, give generously, seek the good of others over self and watch God take you into another dimension in your relationship with Him.

Never say you don't have what to give. I believe strongly that everyone has something to give. You don't have to equate giving to money. God gave His best and it wasn't money! You have time to give, you have love to give, a smile here, a kind word, give encouragement for the weary and many more. I always say, the poorest in the world have something to give. Never let the physical define your giving.

Giving is the act of love. It is inspired by God's unconditional love for us. As we approach the fullness of time concerning the prophetic word in our lives, remember to remain in position – accepting His word, being tenacious and holding on to the word.

Prayer:

Father, spread your love abroad in my heart by your Holy Spirit that I may show forth your love to all. I ask in the name of our Lord Jesus. Amen.

Charge:

Reflect on 1 Corinthians 13. Let us not love as the world does – conditionally. Let us, instead, love as God has shown us! Give your best!

THE HAND OF THE LORD IS UPON YOU

Discovering the various expressions of God

I have been studying the various expressions of power used by God to achieve His ultimate purpose. I have decided to write about the hand of God, sharing with you what happens when the good hand of the Lord comes upon us. I am using three quick examples of persons that have experienced this outpour of power from God.

> *"The Hand of the Lord was upon me, and carried me out in the spirit of the Lord, and set me down in the midst of the valley which was full of bones,"* **Ezekiel 37:1 (KJV)**

The Hand of God is an expression of power that brings about miracles. The Hand of God brings about a "speaking" anointing. Let's look at the Ezekiel example. God asks the prophet to speak to the dry bones, he does, and they become a great army.

The power to speak in this case births life in dead

situations and releases power for the miraculous. What a marvelous thing!

The second example is Nehemiah:

> *And may I have a letter to Asaph, keeper of the royal park, so he will give me timber to make beams for the gates of the citadel by the temple and for the city wall and for the residence I will occupy? And because the gracious hand of my God was on me, the king granted my requests.* **(Nehemiah 2:8 NIV)**

Nehemiah had a great burden in his heart to rebuild the walls of Jerusalem. In Chapter 1, he had been praying, and then in Chapter 2, he was before the king and requested for several things. Because the good hand of the Lord was on him, the king granted him all he asked for.

The third example is Mary the mother of Jesus. She was visited by the Angel Gabriel who informed her of what was to be and told her that the hand of the Lord will be on her.

> *When the angel entered her home, he greeted her and said, "You are favoured by the Lord! The Lord is with you."* ***Luke 1:28***

Like never before, in these times, we need the Hand of God upon us as we walk daily in His will. It is power released to the believer to thrive, live a life of victory and

faith. It makes us bold to accomplish the God-things and to be an instrument to achieve God's agenda.

What sets you apart as a believer? What made these men and women different? The answer is simple: Power! The Hand of God! The Hand of God is the only thing that gives you an edge as a believer. *For by strength shall no man prevail*. **I Samuel. 2:9 (KJV)**

Prayer:

Lord, I pray for Your good hand upon me. Open my eyes to see as You see and to hear You expressly. Give me an obedient heart that I may please You, Father.

Charge:

Therefore, humble ourselves under the mighty hand of God so He will lift you up!

THE MIGHTY ARM OF GOD

Praise be to God from whom every great blessing flows. We should constantly count our blessings rather than the things we are yet to achieve. For the gift of life alone, our thanksgiving should never cease. God is good. He is forever gracious and generous towards His children. Focus on your blessings and gives thanks. The Lord is working out everything for your good. I pray ***God's good hand*** rests on you and gives you power to keep believing, keep speaking and remain in the center of His will.

> *He has performed mighty deeds with his arm; he has scattered those who are proud in their inmost thoughts.* **Luke 1:51 (NIV)**

God's Mighty Arm delivers, His Mighty Arm saves, His Mighty Arm works wonders. The scriptures present us with real life accounts about the children of Israel being saved by God's Mighty Arm. This is an expression of His power over His chosen ones. The stories always depict a situation of hopelessness, trouble, longing for God's

intervention in a matter, etc. God's Mighty Arm (an expression of His awesome power) creates a cycle of what I call the three Rs in the deliverance, salvation or liberation process: **release, restoration and rest.**

He initiates a **release** from captivity. The scriptures speaks about release from a place, deliverance from a place of oppression and captivity. Then the Lord brings you into a place of promise. This is where **restoration** starts. The Lord starts to restore to you what you have lost and more. As the Lord restores, He brings you into a place of **rest**. A place of rest is a place of glory, a place of thanksgiving, a place of multiplication of what he has restored, a place of safety and a place where you are secure in the knowledge that God is for and with you.

Let me encourage you that the Lord is near to all those who call on Him. If you are in a rough place, or tight situation, hold on, the time for release has come. We may not know the process of release, but trust in God whose **Arm** is **Mighty** to save.

Prayer (Thanksgiving):

Father, I give you thanks for Your loving kindness. I am thankful for Your grace and great power upon my life. To You be all the glory. Amen.

Charge:

Exercise your power and authority.

THE MIGHTY ARM OF GOD – RELEASE

Greetings in God's Mighty name! Today, we will study the expression of God's power through His **Mighty Arm in the three R's** – release, restore and rest. I hope to create a paradigm shift with our focus on the first "R" - RELEASE.

Typical stories of release from captivity always speak about a "deliverer". God always uses a person to liberate His people from captivity, whether we speak of Moses, Esther, Nehemiah or our greatest continuous example, Jesus! These stories often used point to a chosen one and specifically a member of the race/people to be delivered out of captivity. However, today, I want to emphasise the fact that our Lord God will use whoever He desires to bring about our release in this new season.

Now it came to pass in the thirty-seventh year of the captivity of Jehoiachin king of Judah, in the twelfth month, on the twenty-fifth day of the month, that Evil-Merodach king of Babylon, in the first year of his reign, lifted up the head of Jehoiachin king of Judah and brought him out of prison. ***Jeremiah 52:31*** **(NKJV)**

We see from this passage that the Bible places a prefix before a king's name like you will put a Mr, Miss or Mrs. The king is being aptly defined so you make no mistake interpreting otherwise. Jehoiachin and others were held for 37 years. 37! An evil king comes into government and within a year releases him and gives him a place of honour and a pension for life! (Read from verses 31-34)

In other words, release for the captured King of Judah came from an unexpected person; God used an evil king. You need to stop praying for your enemies to fall and die because you could just kill off the very person God wants to use to release you into a place of restoration! Funny, isn't it? But King David understood this when in Psalm 23:5a, he said to God, "You prepare a table before me in the presence of my enemies." God will use anyone and anything to bring about a release. Don't be focused on the situation, be focused on God. "Looking unto Jesus who for the joy set before Him endured the Cross..." (paraphrased).

Are you in a rut? Underpaid, overworked? Stuck

with a nasty boss, or have had a promotion denied? Maybe you can't seem to find a job or you are going through rough business conditions. There might be so many bills to pay, or recurring mistakes that threaten your relationship with God. Don't lose faith. There is a joy set before you. Look to Jesus. He is near. He is bringing about your release! He will use whoever He desires to bring you out. Don't start looking for people who could be responsible for your problems. Allow God deal with them! Look to JESUS!

Be steadfast in your walk with God, believe His word, remain hopeful! Your release has come! God is breaking asunder every prison gates of wickedness, delay, sickness, hardship and oppression holding your life.

Prayer (Thanksgiving):

Father, I am thankful for your mighty arm that saves. I am thankful that You are able to do exceeding abundantly above what I can ever ask for or even think. I worship and adore You Lord! I praise Your Holy name.

Charge:

Be thankful. Your enemies will become agents in the hand of God that will take you to your next level of joy.

THE MIGHTY ARM OF GOD – RESTORE

Our Lord and Saviour, Jesus Christ, was sent by the Father to restore man back to his rightful place with Him. In this session, we will look at the "Restore" part of the **Mighty Arm of God** series. Remember we are in the seasons of release, restore and rest.

The release brings you to a new season and a new place of assignment where God starts to restore what has been lost or taken from you in the place of captivity. God wants to give you double for all of the trouble you have gone through. Your pain becomes the power that keeps you in Him.

> *So I will restore to you the years that the swarming locust has eaten, the crawling locust, the consuming locust and the chewing locust.* **Joel 2:25a (NKJV)**

This must be the most popular verse when it comes to restoration after release. God speaks to us about resto-

ration. It's a promise. He will never fail on any promise, He is a good God.

When the God of restoration visited Abraham, he became a father of many nations. *As for me, this is my covenant with you: You will be the father of many nations.* **Genesis 17:4**

When He visited Job, his lost fortunes were restored and God granted him the grace to forgive and pray for his friends, even those that hurt him. After that, the Lord increased all that Job had twofold **(Job 42:10)**. Hannah gave birth to Prophet Samuel after many years of waiting and heartbreak. Her waiting and restoration were clear for all to see.

The key in all restoration stories is our relationship with God. This is the foundation for any journey of restoration any individual takes in life. God restores His relationship with us through Jesus Christ. In that single action of love, all we have lost through sin and unrighteousness is restored to us in Christ. What a delight to know!

My heartfelt prayer today is that the Lord God almighty will restore to you all you may have lost and surprise you with multiple increase. In Jesus' name. Amen!

Prayer:

I praise you Lord for the promise of restoration.

Charge:

Have you accepted Christ as your Lord and Saviour? Be restored to your rightful place with the Father by receiving Christ into your heart. It's as simple as "ABC". Pray with me:

A: Lord Jesus, I ***accept*** you as my personal Lord and Saviour. I denounce all other gods. I declare there is no one else above you.

B: I **believe** You are the Son of God and that You died for my sins to set me free.

C: I **confess** all my sins and ask that Your blood that was shed for me washes my sins away. I will live for You and You alone!

Amen! Congratulations! The most important part of your restoration has just begun!

THE MIGHTY ARM OF GOD – REST

God's mighty hand guides us to a place of rest in Him. He is ever faithful. As we look at the final aspect of God's mighty hand – rest – count your blessings. It completely changes your outlook on life. Remember we are in the seasons of release, restore and rest. Keep the faith, God is near!

Rest is defined as "to cease from work or movement in order to sleep, relax or recover strength."

> *So there is a special rest still waiting for the people of God. For all who have entered into God's rest have rested from their labours, just as God did after creating the world. So let us do our best to enter that rest.* **Hebrews 4:9-11 (NLT)**

God entered His rest after creating the earth. He invites us to come into that rest. When there is a release (from tough times), He restores, then He brings us into a place of rest in Him.

The place of rest is where God's glory is revealed. It is a place of thanksgiving, a place of peace and tran-

quility, a place where you cease from your struggles, a place of multiplication, a place of safety, a place where you KNOW that God is for you. So the question is: how do we get into this place of rest?

Being committed to a deep relationship with God through His Son and trusting Him through the ups and downs of life's journey eventually brings you to a place of rest. How? You finally let go and let God! You know He is handling the situation and that He's got you! You stop struggling, knowing that He that brought about your release and restoration, will grant you a peace that passes all human understanding that will keep your mind and heart stayed on Christ.

Prayer:

Lord, I am thankful for Your grace and peace. I desire to come into Your rest. In Jesus' name. Amen.

Charge:

I charge you to reflect on the God of peace – our Heavenly Father. Be comforted knowing that you are precious to Him. Be thankful. Praise Him. Come into His rest.

FAITH

Now faith is confidence in what we hope for
and assurance about what we do not see.

HEBREWS 11:1 (NIV)

RISE, GO ON YOUR JOURNEY!

The journey of life is about purpose. It is also about representing the One who has sent us. It is a privilege and an honour to serve our God while on this journey of life; being called from assignment to assignment to enhance and advance God's kingdom agenda. However, the sad news is that many of us are yet to start this journey of purpose. Yes! A large number of us have allowed fear to take hold of our hearts and we have remained at point A. Today, I am charging you to rise and step into your God ordained purpose.

> *Rise, take your journey and cross over the River Arnon. Look, I have given into your hand Sihon the Amorite, king of Heshbon, and the land. Begin to possess it, and engage him in battle.* **Deuteronomy 2: 24(NKJV)**

We remain stagnant, not because some enemy somewhere is stopping our journey but because we are not willing to move. We sit in one place moaning about how life has dealt harshly with us. We imagine the enemy to

be big and furious, thinking he will attack us if we went close enough to the land of our desires. In our text, God is commanding His children to move! They had wandered in the wilderness for forty years and it was time to make a move.

What is holding you from taking your journey? Rise! Step into your destiny! God has gone ahead of you. He has made every crooked path straight. He has brought down every mountain of opposition. He has raised up every valley. He has given the enemy into your hands, so go into the land and possess it. You are strong, mighty and God has made you into a mighty weapon to shatter the enemy. Yes, the land is there for the taking.

Prayer:

Today, Lord, open my eyes to see the journey You have designed for me. I receive strength to step into my destiny. In Jesus' name. Amen.

Charge:

GO! GO! GO!

BEING SPECIFIC WITH GOD

Every waking moment of our lives is an opportunity to praise God for another day. Each new day comes with new promises. Unwrap it with joy. Delight in the Father's promises for the day and be THANKFUL! Make declarations. Be specific about what you want. As you make your requests to the Father with a thankful and expectant heart, remember that God dislikes vain repetitions. Be specific about what you desire and He will weed out the selfish desires in you. He will bring you to a place where your desires and His are intertwined, so all that you desire will be His will for you in Christ Jesus.

Now when he had said these things, He cried with a loud voice, "Lazarus, come forth!" **John 11:43*(NKJV)***

Lazarus, brother of Mary and Martha, loved by Jesus, had died from an illness and was buried in the tomb. Jesus arrived four days after his death and raised Lazarus from the dead. I have often heard and believe that if Jesus had just said, "Come forth" without being specific, every

dead person in that city would have been raised. However, Jesus was specific in what He asked His Father for. He asked for Lazarus.

Many examples in the Bible show God's specificity in requesting for offerings and sacrifices, even to the extent of prescribing what the priests were required to wear. In relating with kings, God was very clear in His instructions about battle strategies and dealing with sin. Jesus was specific too. He was specific in asking those desiring a miracle what they wanted. Blind Bartimaeus when brought to Jesus was asked what he wanted. Jesus didn't assume that because he was blind, sight would be priority. We should learn from this and be specific with God. It breeds an honest relationship with Him and also releases faith for a purpose filled life!

Prayer:

Holy Spirit, teach me how to be specific with the Father. In the mighty name of Jesus Christ I pray. Amen!

Charge:

Come into a new dimension of your relationship with the Father. Be specific in your requests and conversations. Let Him know how you feel – pain, worry, anger, depression, your financial and emotional needs. Release faith as you speak to the Father and let Him touch your heart and lead you on the way you should go.

YOU – RELOADED DAILY

Greetings, beautiful one of the Most High God! You are created in God's image and likeness. You are created for good works. You are created for great exploits. You are a giant killer and a Jericho destroyer. You can do ALL things through Christ. You are light and salt; you are more than a conqueror! Praise the Lord!

Blessed be the Lord, who daily loadeth us with benefits, even the God of our salvation. Selah. **Psalm 68:19 (KJV)**

Our God daily loads us with benefits. Think about the word "daily". Every day is new. Every day brings with it new mercies, new territories to conquer, promises to experience and exploits to do. Daily, our God loads us with benefits. Benefits are described as "an advantage or profit gained from something". Another translation describes benefits as "an act of kindness, help that promotes well-being". So, I have personally translated Psalm 68:19 to mean: "Blessed be my Lord who **daily** gives me an advantage over ALL things."

Blessed be my Lord who **daily** gives me profit from all I do.

Blessed be my Lord who **daily** shows me His loving kindness.

Blessed be my Lord who **daily** helps me.

Blessed be my Lord who **daily** promotes my well-being.

Yes. The God of salvation.

Selah.

Get up, people, and give God some crazy praise. We lack no good thing. He daily reloads us. You wake up reloaded, roaring to go and take the day. He has refueled you with power. Bless His Holy Name! He is a good God.

Prayer:

Psalm 103 – Bless the Lord, oh my soul: and all that is within me, bless His Holy Name. Bless the Lord, oh my soul and forget not His benefits.

Charge:

Press in with praise. Things may seem tough but you are reloaded every day! You will win because you have God and you are living under His everlasting benefits scheme.

HOPE

"For God wanted them to know that the riches and glory of Christ are for you Gentiles, too. And this is the secret: Christ lives in you. This gives you assurance of sharing his glory."

COLOSSIANS 1:27 (NLT)

THE CROWD SITUATION

Blind Bartimaeus was a desolate man who was dependent on alms. He barely managed to get by each day and may have felt that life held no promise. He was led out by sunrise to his begging corner and led home by sunset. I believe he must have wondered if there will ever be an end to this meaningless cycle.

> *And when he heard it was Jesus of Nazareth, he began to cry out and say, "Jesus, Son of David, have mercy on me!" Then many warned him to be quiet, but he cried out all the more, "Son of David, have mercy on me!* **Mark 10: 47-48 (NKJV)**

One day he hears a commotion, a crowd is coming, and as they draw near he hears the chants: Jesus! Jesus! His emotions are stirred: Is that Jesus – the miracle worker from Nazareth? This could be his chance to finally get help. So he cries out but the crowd shuts him up. He is an embarrassment, a shameful sight to behold; Jesus shouldn't be concerned with such nonsense. Not

ashamed and not bothered, (after all he had nothing to lose) he cries out again and again and again, until he gets Jesus' attention and gets healed. Alleluia!

Some situations in life bring shame, embarrassment, mockery and dishonour. You may be wondering whether things will ever get better. I have good news: Jesus is passing by! Cry out to him. Don't let the situations drown out your cry or shut you up from calling out to Him. The crowd effect of situations can mute our voices and withhold us from our timely deliverance. CRY OUT! Get his attention and get delivered!

Prayer:

Jesus, I might not be worthy! I may be broken but I know you can heal me. People say I am worthless, I don't stand a chance, but Jesus I'm calling you. Help me Jesus! Deliver me by your outstretched arm.

Charge:

Psalm 145:18a – *The Lord is near to all who call upon Him*. Don't let the intimidation from the crowd of challenges shut down your cry for help! Go on, cry out now: Jesus have mercy on me!

THE HOUSE OF MOURNING

The Bible in Ecclesiastes 7:2 says, "It is better to go to the house of mourning than to go to the house of feasting, for that is the end of all men and the living will take it to heart." Losing loved ones can be traumatic, especially when it's sudden and you don't get a chance to say goodbye. If you have lost someone recently or you are still grieving for a loved one, be comforted by these three things:

> *But I do not want you to be ignorant, brethren, concerning those who have fallen asleep lest you sorrow as others who have no hope. For if we believe that Jesus died and rose again, even so God will bring with Him those who sleep in Jesus.* **I Thessalonians 4:13-14(NKJV)**

We will see them again. The scripture above comforts us with the hope of seeing our loved ones who have died in the Lord. The key phrase there is "died in the Lord." The pain of separation is intense and it is best to take it

one day at a time, but we cannot mourn like we have no hope. The Message Translation says we shouldn't carry on like people who have nothing to look forward to, as if the grave were the last word! If you read all the way down to verse 18, it gives you a further assurance of the resurrection of the dead at the second coming of Jesus Christ. This has been my consolation and comfort.

Jesus knows and feels our grief. Remember that the Lord knows exactly what we are passing through and walks this journey of mourning with us, assuring us of His unfailing love and His comforting Spirit. The Bible tells us in Hebrews 4:15 that Jesus is in touch with our emotions. He understands and has gone through these various situations. He knows exactly what you are going through. He is walking you through the grief because He has been there before.

Lastly, you are a vessel to be used by God. 2 Corinthians 1:4-5 (MSG) says, "God of all healing counsel! He comes alongside us when we go through hard times, and before you know it, he brings us alongside someone else who is going through hard times so that we can be there for that person just as God was there for us." So don't waste your pain! Use it to bless others. That's God's ultimate purpose.

Prayer:

Lord, today I thank you for blessing me with *(insert loved one's name)* and the opportunity of knowing and loving her/him. Thank you for the comfort through the Holy Spirit in this time of mourning. I receive your love. In Jesus' name. Amen.

Charge:

Comfort one another through trials and affliction. Today, seek out someone going through something you have gone through and comfort them with the comfort that God has given/shown you.

ACKNOWLEDGEMENTS

To Dad and Mum: thank you both for being my rock. Dad, though you have gone to be with the Lord, I hear and feel you daily. You never left.

To my siblings, Baba, Nkoko, Doc and AK, thank you for evergreen memories and ever-present ones.

To Ndidi Nwuneli, you gave me the idea for this book on my fortieth birthday. I had started a blog in 2015 out of a place of restlessness and you encouraged me to start putting it all together in a book. The book is finally here. Thank you Didi. To Udo, Sophia, Barbie, Tito, Buki, Adaobi, you shape my world in many ways you don't even realise. Thank you for being my soul sisters.

To my families at This Present House, The Father's Church and Wellspring of Life, I love you more than words can express. Thank you for your love.

To Uche, Blossom, Paya and the entire crew, thank you for your help and encouragement. The long hours paid off.

To those on the journey of life – keep at it!

ABOUT THE AUTHOR

Ogechukwu Funlola Modie is a writer, public speaker and radio/television host. She is the founder of Kairos Knowledge Centre, a youth capacity building organisation and the First Born Founda-

tion, whose core mission is to daily contribute to the overall wellbeing of individuals. She writes weekly on her blogs, www.wellspringoflifeinternational.com and www.heelsofinfluence.com.

Modie's career spans Corporate Finance, SME ventures, Private Equity, Opinion Research and most recently Public Policy and Administration where she has held senior executive roles. She has won diverse awards for her work on leadership, philanthropy and mentorship. A certified project manager, her current role as the Chief of Staff to the Minister of State Petroleum Resources has seen her manage key reform programs in the Nigerian Oil and Gas Sector.

She is passionate in advocating for causes on gender rights, youth development, and rights for people living with disabilities. She sits on various boards, including Affirm Consulting, an organisation with focus on women and youth rights; Victorious Women; Cedar Seed Foundation, with special focus on advocating for the rights of women and the disabled in the society; and Noon Day, which advocates in the area of the rehabilitation of Internally Displaced Persons (IDPs).

Born in Ibadan and raised in Enugu, Oge has a degree in Economics from the University of Nigeria Nsukka and a Masters in Business from the Cranfield University, United Kingdom. Oge resides in Abuja, Nigeria and volunteers in her free time to work on community projects.

To Jesus, the Well that can never run dry.